The Childrei.

A Male perspective on dealing with abortion

1.

The Abortion

These days, websites, organizations, support groups are all set up to help women through the tough decision to have an abortion. These groups help before, during and after the procedure. They are meant to soften the blow, help support the woman emotionally, especially since in many cases the men simply take off as soon as the woman mentions pregnancy. Even though a man can never hold a candle to a woman's pain and anguish both before and after an abortion, some men, real men, do feel pain with abortion. Some men are chicken hearted, they only care about themselves, they can't be bothered with pregnancy, no matter what the woman decides to do, these are shameful men whom I have no respect for. Of course none of the pain a man feels is physical, but more psychological and emotional. The man loses a possible child, just like the woman does. I went through this, in two different instances. Years later I still feel the pain. Today I have a son that is 20 and who I am very proud of, however, I should also have a 17 and 18 year old. I am still not sure all these years later, whether I made the right decision or not. Although it has been a long time, I still find myself haunted by the memories that never existed, the kids I never had, and the good or bad events that never took place. I have spent more than one sleepless night thinking about such things, I can only imagine what the women must go through as well. I cherish life, I have spent most of my life helping others, maybe that will make up for this, I'm not sure. I have not told my son about the brothers or sisters he may have had, it's painful for me to think about, why make it painful for him as well? Anyway, this is my story about my children that never were.

2.

The nanny

Back in my playboy days as a single fireman in a small town, I bounced around a lot, one apartment to the next, never really putting down roots for long. I was always looking for the cheapest deal, I actually started my adult life living on a couch in a house owned by two older females. It was the perfect price, free! My duties were simply to watch the 4 children of these women, who ranged in age from 3-9 years old, all females. It worked well until I woke up one morning and found all 4 of them outside in the snow, in nothing but pajamas. Of course as the responsible adult, I ran outside after them, they split up, ran into the house, and locked me outside in the snow. There I stood, in the snow, no shoes, in boxers and a tee shirt, shivering and shaking, staring into the window as these little devils ran amuck throughout the house. After 30 minutes or so in 10 degree weather, the 3 year old finally came to the sliding glass door and asked,

"Do you want to come in now? You look cold." She asked, with her beautiful blue eyes looking up at me.

"Yes, please, and you won't get in any trouble, just your sisters." I uttered through quivering lips.

"No, get away from the door, let him stay out there!" The nine year old yelled.

"Don't listen to her; she is the devil, dressed as a nine year old girl." I said, as I exchanged sneers with the eldest child.

"But his face is blue, and he is shivering, and he said I won't get into trouble for the mess." She said, as she unlocked the door.

I entered the house, and everyone got a time out, well, those that listened to me, which was only the 3 year old, the one I told didn't have to get in time out.

"It's ok sweetie, you don't get time out remember, you don't have to stand in the corner." I said, as I ran my fingers through her hair.

"But I feel sorry for you, the other kids don't care what you say, so I will Mr. Tom guy." She said, as she turned towards the corner for her time out.

As I stood before this disaster that once was the front room of this house, I then realized that being an 18 year old nanny, was probably not my calling in life. Not to mention things got a little weird when I ended up in bed with one of the ladies that lived in the house. It was better than sleeping on the couch, but still was not for a swinging single guy like me. I had an offer to move in with a friend who was a motorcycle racer, and a partying wild man like me. We got along well till he slept with my girlfriend, we had our power turned off, and I spent the extremely cold winter in a house with no electricity, no gas, and no car after wrecking my vehicle on a drunken evening. After my father saved the day and helped me get back on my feet, I lived with my grandmother for a short time.

3.

Tara

After living with my grandmother for a time, I needed to get back to my single life, I found myself living in a large house with several roommates. The old house had been an 18th century stagecoach stop, it looked like it too, it creaked and made noises, the lady who owned the house told me it was haunted.   Well I am not sure about all that. The house had 7 bedrooms, mine was the smallest, no closet, no insulation, it was an added on room, poorly done I might add. The other rooms were rented to young adults around my age, including a girl who slept in the room next to mine, her name was Tara. Tara was a friendly outgoing girl, like myself, she was always in and out, we didn't see each other much for the first few months, just a hi and bye in passing. One day I accidently caught a glimpse of her coming out of our community bathroom shower naked. She was startled; but didn't seem too concerned, judging by the smile on her face. A few days later I passed her in the hall and said,

"Hey Tara, sorry about the other day, I didn't mean to walk in on you."

"Oh well, it's not your fault, I didn't keep the door locked, hope you enjoyed the view." She said, with a smirk on her face.

"Yes in fact I did." I replied.

"I might have to accidently walk in on you sometime." She said.

"Well we can work on that, why don't we start with meeting for a drink tomorrow night?" I suggested.

"Sounds like a plan Tom, or should I call you Tom Cat. "She said, "Pick me up at my room at 7 sharp."

"Alright then, it's a date." I said.

Since the night before my 'sneak out girl' had paid me a late night visit, I call her my 'sneak out' girl because she was 18 and still living with her parents, she would sneak out a few times a week to come roll around in bed with me. I'm sure Tara heard her and I till all hours of the night, so I doubted she would want to turn our drink date into a sexual rendezvous. I was mistaken. She asked me who was in my room the night before, and what all the noise was, then she told me she was jealous of the noises. After our drinks loosened us up a bit, we made our way back to my room that night and she made louder noises than my 'sneak out girl'.

We made a nightly habit of this for several weeks; my 'sneak out girl' was put on the back burner, which bummed her out. She came over one night and tapped on my window, only to hear Tara and I in bed, I heard her swearing at me as she left.

It was about 6 weeks after our relations began that Tara entered my room one evening, as white as a ghost, she had been throwing up all day, and her stomach was hurting.

"Tom, I might be pregnant." She muttered.

"Huh? How's this possible, I thought you were on the pill?" I remarked.

"Well it's very possible. But before I told you I wanted to make certain, so I bought a home pregnancy test, it is sitting on the counter in the bathroom right now, we have a few minutes before we are supposed to check it. Do you want to check it or shall I?" She said, teary eyed.

"I guess both of us huh?" I replied.

"Ok, I guess I can handle that." She said as she led me by the hand towards the bathroom.

I felt a range of emotions, a baby, what should I do? I already had one child that I barely spent time with; he scared the hell out of me, what if it was a girl? Oh my god, what the hell will I do with a girl? Neither of us were ready for a child, I worked for minimum wage in retail and as a part-time, poorly paid fireman; she was a part time massage therapist. What business do we have bringing a child into this mess?

"We are pregnant." Tara said, as she looked down at the test in front of me.

"Really? Are you sure? Maybe your pee is lying." I nervously spouted, as I grabbed the test and shook it. Hoping the two blue lines would form one.

"Ha-ha, no Tom, I am pregnant." She said, with a smile and a chuckle.

I looked up at her, her face was gleaming, I couldn't splash reality on her right now, I wanted her to enjoy the moment. I must admit, I enjoyed it for a minute as well.

"What are we gonna do, we aren't even in a relationship yet? My mother is going to have a fit." Tara said, as she exited the bathroom, anxiety beginning to set in.

"I don't know Tara. We will have to talk some more about this, but for now, let's just enjoy this moment." I said, as I hugged her tightly.

Her mother, who owned the house we lived in, was a crazy lady. We knew she was mentally unstable, she would sit in her room and watch faith healing all day, she was not fit to raise our child. Tara's brother also lived in the same house, and was not in a position either; he was a homosexual man trying to survive in a small conservative, intolerant town not meant for him. I told Tara I would leave this decision up to her and that I would support whatever decision she makes. She was a beautiful young woman who had hopes and dreams as I did; she was not ready for motherhood.

Tara came to me about a week later, we had barely spoken in that uncomfortable week, her mother ignored me and all but kicked me out of the house when she did speak. She blamed me for all of it. She also knew about the ladies I had in and out of my room on a daily basis, she knew I was not good for her daughter and rightfully so. My 'day sneak out girl' came for a visit that week when Tara's mother was home, she made a few comments about me when we tried to exit the house. I call her my 'day sneak out girl' because she was married with kids, she waited till her husband went to work, and her kids to school, then she would sneak over to my house.

"You are a whore Tom, isn't it enough you knocked my daughter up? Hey lady, do you know about this guy? He's a sleaze ball! You need to get out of my house, both of you!" She said.

Tara left me a note on my door one morning. It read: "Could you please clear out your bedroom tonight, I will be home around 6 and we need to talk, apologize to your dates you probably have planned for tonight, but this is important. Tara."

I don't know how she knew, but I did have a date that night, but I cancelled, 6pm came fast it seemed, there was a knock at my door. Tara entered with a very solemn look on her face.

"We can't keep this kid Tom." Tara said, as she sat on my bed. "This kid would have a broken home right off the bat, it would not be right. I am in no position, and neither are you. Just and FYI, my mother knows I want an abortion, she is totally against it, she wants to raise the kid as her own. I don't think she could handle it, I wouldn't want her too. "

I sat and stared for a moment, letting this new turn of events sink in. "Well Tara, I told you it was your decision, I back you whatever you decide." I said, as I caressed her face, and wiped a tear from her cheek. "Just be sure, please, is this what you really want? There is no second chance, no going back."

"No Tom, this is not what I want, but it's not about you and me, it's about this child and the life it would not have, the life we could not give it. It is the right thing to do. So my answer is, yes, let's do this."

"Ok, we will, I will pay for it, be there for it, the whole thing."

"I'm not so sure I want you there, it may be a hard thing for you to go through, it's gonna be hell for me" Tara said.

"No, I will be there, hard or not, this is our child, it can only be this way. I stand behind the decisions in my life." I replied, sternly.

"Alright, I appreciate it." Tara said, falling into my arms.

4.

My son

We attended the first appointment together a few days later; it was more like a counseling session than a doctor's appointment. The doctor asked us, are there any alternatives? What about my family? My father and mother were divorced, and in no position to raise more kids in their advancing age. My mother was a fierce conservative, if she knew I was even considering such a thing, she was possibly disown me from the family, her parents as well being strict Catholics. My father was a grouchy, old school fireman, he would not support this in any way, but he would not disown me, nor volunteer his parenthood to raise this child. I am an only child; I had neither siblings nor close friends to lean on, or ask to step up. He asked, what about adoption? Tara knew she would have to take off of work sooner than later, a pregnant massage therapist is a tough job; she couldn't miss that much work. As our counseling session continued, it seemed almost like the doctor was trying to talk us out of this, but I suppose this was part of his job. I don't think anyone, even an abortion doctor, is 'pro-abortion', they are just in favor a woman having the right to choose. An appointment for the next week was made for the procedure.

No dates that week, kept everyone away, I needed some solitude to ponder this life changing decision Tara had made. We sat up the night before the procedure in my room, gazing out at the stars; I have not ever forgotten the site we saw that night. It was almost like a sign. Was it a sign we were doing the right thing? Was it a sign we were making a mistake? We both saw a small orange glow deep in the night sky, it moved slowly across the sky, then faded away, we couldn't believe our eyes, and it almost made us change our minds. However, after the orange glow faded, we were still Tom and Tara, two strangers and a would-be baby. We spent that night holding each other close; we made love, and found ourselves tearing up during. We stopped briefly a few times questioning ourselves on whether or not we are making the right decision. Tara would not answer when I asked; simply shake her head, with tears flowing out of her eyes.

"What is we are about to abort the future president?" I asked

"Tom, I know you want this, but you left it up to me, please don't make this any harder, it's killing me" Tara replied.

"I know, I am sorry, I want to be certain we are making the right decision." I said.

"Describe a day in the life of our baby, if you can paint a pretty picture, than we can make this work." Tara replied.

I stopped my sexual actions, rolled off of her, and laid there. What passed through my mind was scary. I began to imagine, what would this be like? I pictured Tara leaving at 6am, heading to her job, myself, waking up a baby; I didn't know how to raise, changing its diapers, having it spit up on me, not knowing how to stop making it cry.

"Come on kid, does anything stop on the way through?" I would say, trying to wipe up all the mess left in his diaper." Sorry your dad is kind of a dummy, I don't know how to make you stop crying, what is wrong little buddy?"

I saw myself picking him up, rocking him back and forth, just to have him spit up all over my work clothes.

"Aww geez kid, what the hell are you doing to me?"

I see Tara walking through the door, "Oh no, you are a mess, what happened?" She asked

"Well I fed him like you said, and he spit up all over me when I started to rock him in my arms."

"Tom, use your head huh, do you want to be rocked right after a meal? Hurry up and get changed, I need to get the baby to the sitter, I have another massage in an hour." She angrily said, as she grabbed the baby and took him to the bathroom.

"Sorry, I don't know what I'm doing here."

"Electrical tape? You put the baby's diaper on with electric tape wrapped around him? What the hell is the matter with you?" Tara yelled from the bathroom.

"Well the stupid tape tabs kept ripping," I replied, putting my head down, "cheap damn diapers."

"No Tom, it's not the diapers, it's you. Start paying attention will ya?" Tara said, as she whizzed by the bedroom, and out the backdoor.

"Good bye," I said as I stood at the backdoor watching her load the baby in the car and peel out. "I guess I don't get to kiss my family good bye huh?"

I imagined Tara getting tired of my immaturity, and kicking me out. My job at the gas station would not pay enough to provide child support; I may find myself a dead beat dad, out on the streets unable to care for my small family. I felt a pain in my chest; it knocked the wind out of me to feel this helpless. I almost felt panicked, then I had another thought. I pictured myself many years later, living on a street corner, eating out of dumpsters, petty stealing to get by, sickly, dying slowly, broke and broken. It's a bright sunny day. The cars are whizzing by, no one notices me, sitting in my pile of filth on the sidewalk, my sign says 'will work for food', although I have not worked in years and I don't plan on it. I'm incognito, I'm unknown, I disappeared, which I thought was best for the family I shamed, that I couldn't support.

I see a young man approaching me; he looks down at me,

"Yes, need something? Got some spare change kid?"

The young man knelt down next me. He is well dressed, groomed nicely, taken care of.

"Are you Tom?" The figure would ask.

"Who wants to know young man?" I would reply, as I scoot back a little, regressing into my small encampment.

"I think I might be your son."

"Son? Which one? I have one I knew about, are you Tara's kid?"

"Yes, that's me."

"Oh, why would you want to find me? I'm no good son, I left you alone and as well as my other son, for both of your own good, please just leave me be." I said, as I reached for my liquor bottle and took a drink. "You look great, well taken care of, what can I possibly do to make your life any better?"

"I thought maybe you would like to be involved in my life now, I'm in high school, captain of the football team, starting my senior year next month, just once in my life I would like for my father to watch me play a game." He said as he sat down next to me.

"Look kid, I don't even know you, I don't even know your name. I left you alone because I was a young man who had a kid that I was unable to take care of, I knew your mother would be capable." I would say, as I looked away from him, finding it hard to look him in the face.

"My mother was killed last summer, it is her mother who is raising me, and she found you somehow and suggested I seek you out."

I gazed off into the sunlight, a tear flowed down my face, I pictured all the love I'm sure Tara had poured on this kid, just so be taken from him way to early. "Tara is dead?" I asked, whipping the tears away, "her crazy mom is raising you? She didn't get you involved in all that faith healing crap did she?"

"Yes she is raising me, with her new husband, she is a wonderful lady, I'm very lucky, she is married to a nice man, and he does what he can, but he is old and can't walk very well." He said, as he put an arm on my shoulder," but he is not my father."

"Kid, neither am I, now please, I have nothing for you, leave me be." I said, as I brushed his arm off of my shoulder. "You would have been much better off if you had never found me, now please go away." I said, as I took another drink from my bottle.

He stood up, gazed down at me. "Ok, if that's how you want it, just remember, you made the choice to bring me into this world, your responsibilities don't stop once you make that choice." He handed me a slip of paper with a phone number. "If you ever change your mind, give me a call."

He would turn and walk away, vanish from my life, leaving me to my despair, and my bottle.

Then I pictured lying in a hospital bed, years later, dying. Barely able to open my eyes, nurses rushing around me, trying to save my old body, after a life of abusing it, trying to perform miracle, to save a man who didn't want to be saved.

"Sir, do you have anyone else we should call? "A nurse would ask.

"Else? Who did you call?" I weakly uttered.

"There was a slip of paper we found in your wallet, it had a number on it, the man who answered said he was your son. He is on his way." She replied.

"Why the hell did you bother him?" I asked, as I raised my voice, coughed, and began to choke from all the fluid in my lungs.

She didn't answer, noises from the monitors started to beep, the nurses and doctors began to gather at my bedside, I felt myself begin to fade. My breathing became more difficult.

"Sir we are going to knock you out and put you on a breathing tube." The doctor standing by my head said.

"NO!" I yelled, I slowly opened my eyes, looked over at the nurse and barely whispered," You said my son is coming right?"

"Yes sir, but you may not be alive by then if we don't put this tube in you." She replied.

"I don't care; I want to see him one more time. I'm a tough old bird, I'll wait. If it's my day to die then so be it, but my son is gonna see his father alive one last time. I have something to tell him." I uttered, as I took a deep breath, and sighed, gurgling coming from my airway.

Right then, a middle aged man approached my bedside, grabbed my hand and whispered, "I'm here for ya dad."

"Son, I'm glad you made it, look I'm heading out, it's my time." I said as I looked into his eyes filled with tears. "I want you to know, I'm sorry I was such a poor excuse for a father, I let you down, and I let your mother down. I am very proud of the man you have grown to be. Your mom is looking at you from above, smiling down I'm sure. "

"Tell her I said hi dad." He whispered as he kissed my forehead.

As I gasped my last breath, never knowing the true joys of fatherhood with either of my kids, never letting my son know I had spied on every home game that year in high school, it took me a few games to find out which player he was, but it was one of the only joys I had experienced in many years. I thought my son would only be embarrassed by his homeless father cheering in the stands, so I took my post where I deserved, under the bleachers, where I slept some nights, and collected food particles dropped from above.

These actions would also end my slim relationship I already had with my current son, whom I saw little, and was very uneasy around. As I thought about this, it became clear that even though this may not be the outcome, it is scary enough to make me agree with the abortion decision.

"Ok Tara, you are right, I won't mention it again." I said, as I rolled over and began to weep lightly.

.5

The Procedure

When morning hit, I woke to see Tara had stayed in her bed that night. I waited for what seemed like an eternity for her to come to my room and get me for our appointment. There was no hug or kiss, simply her opening the door, "let's go." She said.

As we exited the house, her mother ran after, confronting us on the front door steps.

"Today is the day isn't it?" She asked.

"Yes mom, please let us go, we will be late." Tara replied.

"Please reconsider one last time, you used to talk about being a mommy when you were a kid, this isn't like you, it's him! Why did I ever let you enter my home?" She yelled.

"No mom, it is all me, I can't handle this right now, we need to leave."

"Fine, but when you come home Tom, you need to pack your crap, you are outta here!" Tara's mother said.

"Understood maam, and I understand your concerns, but this is her decision." I said, as I walked away.

"Screw you punk, you brainwashed my daughter, you are about to make her murder her child, you are garbage kid!" she screamed as she followed us to the car.

Tara stared back at her mother as I ushered her into the car and we left.

I think that was the longest 5 mile car ride I ever experienced. We arrived at the doctor's office. It seemed very appropriate, quiet, almost like a funeral home. I remember thinking, are we gonna have a funeral today? What do I do with what is left over of my child? Can he feel anything?

My heart began to race, my arms shaking. Tara looked at me, and asked if I was ok.

"Yeah I'm great, just have some questions." I replied, pouring sweat down my brow.

"Tom we had the opportunity to ask questions during the counseling, today is the day, we do this, no turning back." She said, with a strong tone, and a stare into my eyes.

We were brought into a small room, seemed very white and cold, almost something you would see in a horror movie when someone is about to undergo a medical procedure by the bad guy against their will.

There was a large machine in the corner; it had some hoses and chambers attached to it. The doctor entered.

"Young man stand there, next to her and don't look in this direction, direct your eyes towards the painting please."

I thought, maybe this is my only chance to see my child, do I want to miss it? He began the procedure, turned the machine on, Tara squealed, squeezed my hand tightly, tears began to flow down her cheek, as they did mine. She looked up at me, and said, "look at the painting Tom, don't look over here."

"Please sir, look away from this procedure, it's what's best for you. Tara, you as well." The doctor repeated.

This moment took me back a few years to my grandfather's funeral. It was an open casket; he looked amazing, peaceful, and quiet. I was happy to be able to see him one last time. After the funeral, they ushered all of us out of the funeral parlor, I asked my mother, "What do they do with him now mom?"

"Now they close the coffin, and take him to be buried." She replied as she rushed me through the door.

"No, I want to watch them close the casket mom; I want to see him one last time." I said as I stopped walking.

"Tom honey that is a traumatic thing to watch, I don't want you watching that." My mom said as she began to drag me away.

"Geri, I will take him, I want to watch myself, he is 16 years old, he is old enough." Said my grandfather's brother.

"Ok big shot, but don't come crying to me when you have nightmares." She said, as she marched away.

I knew my grandfather would be taken good care of, but I wanted to see that final moment for myself. My uncle and I were the only ones left in the funeral parlor when they rolled up the blanket that had hung on the side of the casket, and placed it over my grandfather. The slowly closed it. My uncle put his arm around me and said, "He is in a better place now Tom." It is one of the very few times my uncle ever talked to me in my life, he was not very friendly, but he showed some emotion and compassion for me at that moment.

Standing next to Tara, knowing this might be the only chance I get to see my kid, even piece of him or her, before the doctor in effect 'closes the coffin', I glanced over at the doctor.

"Look away sir." The doctor said rather angrily.

All I saw was a hose, no signs of my kid. I felt empty inside.

I turned to look at the painting, it was a beautiful landscape, a mountain somewhere, the machine sounded like a vacuum, louder and louder, it frightened me. I could no longer see the landscape, tears blurred my vision. What the hell were we doing? Should we be doing this? Am I allowing someone to kill my child? I turned to Tara and blurted "we can't do this Tara, we simply can't, this isn't right, we have a child together." Tara's tears began to flow down her cheek; she smiled, touched my face, caressed my cheek and whipped my tears away.

Just then the doctor turned off the machine. He looked at both of us, "We are finished here, and the procedure is complete. Please gather your emotions and meet me in the next room."

I was in shock I think, we did it, we aborted our fetus. This is a choice we would have to live with for the rest of our lives.

We went home, silent the whole way, not a word. I began moving my stuff out, rented a small apartment. All the time I spent moving out, I would get constant scowls from Tara's mother, she still blamed me for the whole thing. I let her hate me, it was fine. Tara, the next day, moved her bedroom into the attic, I made a few attempts in the next few weeks to see her, she didn't seem interested. I felt like she was the only link to my child who we aborted. If I let her go, it would be letting go of my child. I found myself trying to spend more time with the son I already had, I cherished the moments with him, but couldn't help but feel sadness when I was with him, never knowing what the child we aborted would have been like.

6.

Dawn

I left Tara's house in the summertime, beautiful time of the year, birds chirping, water in the lake warm and inviting. I flooded my son with attention that summer, even though he was at a point in his life where he wanted his mom, and would cry, sometimes even hiding from me when I came to pick him up. It hurt, but I felt by spending as much time with him as I could, I would make up for the child I let go.

Even though I made a lot of time for my son, I still made my time for playing the field with as many women as I could fit into my schedule. It was a good distraction. I made it a policy to not have these women around my son though. I also never told any of them what I had been through. Occasionally I would have a sleepless night, up crying, having nightmares about what the fetus may have went through during the procedure.

One evening I entered a local gas station, grabbed a bottle of soda and headed towards the counter, I noticed a pretty brunette behind the counter that I had not met before.

"Hello, you must be a new employee." I asked.

"Why yes I am, my name is Cassi." She replied, as she extended her hand.

We exchanged some chit chat, she had just moved here from college, and was staying with her parents in town. She had the cutest laugh and smile; I had to see her again.

"Maybe we could get together sometime?" I asked

"Awww, I would love that, but I am seeing someone." She replied, dipping her bottom lip. I could feel an attraction between us, but as a player, I had two options break down the wall, or walk away. Just before I made my decision she said," But, my friend Dawn would like you I think, we have the same taste. You're a cutie."

I thought, hmmm, a blind date, I have been there before, can be scary. Cassi gave me a brief description, sounded perfect, which back then meant, hot and local. That was my loose criteria, being broke meant I had no money to travel to see women.

"Ok, hook me up Cassi, I am gonna trust you, if she is not a good blind date, than I am gonna march back here and steal you from your boyfriend. Deal?"

She laughed, "Ok deal!"

Cassi wrote down my number, and told me Dawn would call me.

Since my social calendar was pretty full, I was not too concerned about whether or not I received this phone call.

5 or 6 days later, my phone rings. "Hello." I said

"Is this Tom?" the cute voice on the phone asks.

"This is, who is this?"

"My name Is Dawn, Cassi told me to call you, she is trying to fix me up. I swear she can't accept that I like being single. Haha." She said.

"Really, then why did you call me?" I replied.

"Well she said you are really cute, and life is boring right now on the days I don't have my son."

Oh yeah, I thought, this will be a walk in the park, a bored, vulnerable mommy, what could be better.

We made plans for me to pick her up the next night; she was living at her grandmother's house, helping her out in her advanced age. She had a child, a 2 year old. She didn't have him living there much though, which always gives me pause for thought, but this was slated to just be a one nighter, so I wasn't worried.

We went out to dinner, headed to a bar near my house for a few drinks. Then we headed to my house and right into bed, where we stayed for most of the weekend. We were very attracted to each other, and we clicked sexually.

After that weekend, I kinda thought about her, and wanted to see her more, she seemed reluctant.

"Wasn't this just a one nighter for you Tom?" she said on the phone, when I asked to see her again. "I already heard all about you, bet you can find another woman to hang with tonight."

"Come on Dawn, don't believe everything you hear. It is only a one nighter if we decide for it to be. I had fun, didn't you?" I replied, pulling out my slick lines, well I thought they were slick.

"I will think about it, call you later." She said as she hung up.

She didn't call back. Why was this little Philly blowing me off? I'm the blow off guy; I was not used to this. I tried a few more times that week to contact her, no answer, no call back.

After two weeks of no answers to my calls, I showed up at her grandmother's house, a very unusually aggressive move for me. She was there alone.

"I guess you didn't get the hint huh Tom?" She said, after opening the door.

"Look I just want to talk for a few minutes, are you alone?"

"Yes, come in I guess." She said, as she let me in.

It was a hot muggy day, and only a few minutes after entering the room, we were naked on the floor of her grandmother's living room, hot sweaty, and wild. I had no idea what we were about to do.

I thought for sure I had her locked up; I liked her and wanted more than a one or two nighter. After a few hours, I left. She seemed smiling and happy, like she was into seeing me again soon

Sure enough, I made a few attempts to contact her that week, but she declined to answer. I saw Cassi at the gas station, and she said Dawn had not been feeling good.

Dawn finally called me back after a few more weeks of no contact, and said we needed to meet up and talk. She couldn't give me a reason for the cold shoulder since our hot sweaty day on her grandmother's floor, weeks before. We made plans to meet at a bar that weekend.

I was excited to see her, it had been almost 6 weeks since we saw each other, I was hoping to have a drink then back to my place. I sat there in that chair for an hour and half, she never showed. I asked the bartender if anyone called asking for Tom. He said there had been no calls. I sat drinking my soda in silence. After 2 hours, I got up and left in shame.

Since my social calendar was still pretty full, I decided I would write her off, and move on as I commonly did. No big deal. Then, a few weeks later, she called me.

"We need to meet Tom." She said, as soon as I picked up the phone.

"Oh, like we were supposed to do last month?" I replied, in an upset tone. "Don't waste my time lady."

"I am very sorry I stood you up, it won't happen again, let's meet tomorrow, ok?" She said

"Why all of a sudden? You getting some thrill outta playing the player? Hey I have feelings too ya know. "I replied.

"No, I promise, I will be there."

"Ok, same place then? 5pm ok? Last chance, you don't show, don't ever call me again, got me?" I asked forcefully, reluctantly, violating all my rules by even talking to this woman.

"Yes, I will see you then." Dawn replied, as she hung up the phone.

Her call didn't alarm me; I thought she was going to tell me how her son's father came back into her life and blablabla, same song and dance I had heard before. I wish it was.

We met the next day, Dawn was actually there before I was, I sat down.

"Hi Tom, let me start by apologizing for the way I have been behaving, but there is a good reason." Dawn said, as she grabbed my hand and stared into my eyes.

"Ok, what is that reason? Let me guess, you kid's poppa is back in town?" I asked

"No, not at all, I would never take that guy back, he is garbage. "She replied, "This is much different."

"Ok, so shoot, let's not beat around the bush, why did you stand me up?" I asked as I pulled my hand away and sat back in my chair.

"Tom, I wanted to meet you last time to ask you what to do about a situation in my life, but I chose to make the decision myself, without any input from anyone else." She said, as she looked down, a tear rolling down her cheek. "Tom I was pregnant, and I didn't know what to do, so I aborted the child without telling you."

Wow, it all raced back, Tara, my son, the street corner, the death bed I laid on, the football games I watched from under the bleachers. She did this without me knowing, I had no say.

"What?" I exclaimed, "How the hell could you make that decision without me?"

"Because Tom, I don't want another kid right now, I couldn't handle it. What kind of life would it have led with you and me barely knowing each other, trying to raise this kid with little money and no help, plus, I already have a kid and so do you, a kid you hardly ever see. What would this kid's life have been like?"

I stared at her, looking almost through her, looking out the window behind her. I saw a little girl, cute, blonde with pigtails; she was riding a pony, with me pulling guiding the pony. She giggled, her blue eyes shined in the sunlight. She looked down at me and said, "This is the best Birthday present ever. Thank you daddy!"

"Glad you like it honey." I replied. "Daddy loves you, don't ever forget that."

"I know daddy, I love you too." The little girl said. "When can you come over and see us at our new house?"

"Well mommy wouldn't like that; I'm not really allowed to be there."

"Why not?" She asked.

"Well mommy's new boyfriend is a cop, and he doesn't seem to like the idea. That's why this lady is here with us today." I replied.

"I don't like mommy's new boyfriend, he is a meanie." The little girl said angrily.

"You and me both honey." I replied.

As I led the pony over to the stable, Dawn pulled up in a car off in the distance, a woman in a business suit walks over to where I am standing and says, "it's time for her to go, your hour is up sir."

"Please just a few more minutes, she is enjoying herself." I replied.

Dawn exits her car and stands next to it staring a hole through me. "Let's Go! The flight leaves in an hour." She yells.

"Sorry sir, she needs to get back home." She says.

"Ok, I know, come here sweetheart." I said, as I helped her off the pony and hugged her in my arms. "Don't ever forget, daddy will love you forever and always, no matter how far away you live."

"I love you too daddy, I'm sorry mommy moved, this has been so hard the past few months not seeing you." She said, as she clutched me, and began to cry.

"Come on princess, let's get a move on!" Dawn yelled from her car.

"Sir, I need to take her now, let's go."

The woman takes her from my shoulder, as she holds onto me for dear life, "No daddy, I don't want to go. Please, mommy's new boyfriend is mean."

The woman carries her to Dawn, they disappear into the car and drive away, I hear my daughter's cries off in the distance, I am standing there with a pony, petting him, drowning in my sorrow.

Then I notice myself, off in another direction, older, gray, aged. I look like a shell of a man. I am walking through a department store, it is Christmas time, I have a small gift in my hand. As I shuffle through the crowds, I am looking for someone. People bumping into me, as I cannot get around easily anymore, I am feeble. I notice a stunning woman standing behind the cosmetics counter. She is a blonde, blue eye, as deep as the ocean. She is primped, and proper, well taken care of. I stand in line, she doesn't look my way. She is cheerful, greeting each of the customers with a smile, and happy banter about the impending holiday. I eventually get up to the counter, she looks up at me.

"Hello sir, Merry Christmas to you, what can I get you today?" This vision of loveliness says to me

"Hi miss; it certainly is a Merry Christmas isn't it? Seems pretty busy in here today." I said, nervously, my hands beginning to shake, my voice crackling.

"Yes it sure is, did you need help finding a gift?" She asked.

"Miss, I already have a present, it's for you." I said, as I handed a small box to her.

"For me? Do we know each other sir?" She asked as she took the present from my hands.

"We met a long time ago ma'am, you were unforgettable." I said.

"Well I have heard that before, are you trying to get a date for this lonely holiday? I am very happily married, just so you know." She said, as she produced a large wedding ring which sat on her finger and shined like a blazing star.

I snickered, "No ma'am, certainly not, no ulterior motives."

She began to open the box, she reaches inside and pulls out a picture, she gasped. She stared down at the picture, a tear rolled down her face.

"My love, I took that picture of you the last time I saw you, when they pulled you off that pony and swept you out of my life."

She looked up at me, "Why did you come here? Are you drunk?" She angrily said.

"No, I had heard of the passing of your mother, and I thought maybe you needed a parent in your life." I said.

"I don't, not one like you, my father is the police chief, successful, well thought of. You are a sperm donor nothing more. My husband is one of his officers; we don't need a drunk like you in our lives." She said as she came from around the counter and got in my face.

"I have not had a drink in 10 years. Why do you keep thinking I am a drunk? What did she tell you about me?" I asked.

"She told me enough, you were an out of work drunk, who hit her which is why she left your sorry butt. She always told me to stay completely away from you."

"Yes, I was a louse at one time, but I cleaned myself up just so I can try and be a part of your life. I also heard you have children; do they know they have a grandfather? "I asked.

"Yes, they have two great sets of grandparents, you do not need to be a part of that, don't even consider trying to contact them, I will have you arrested immediately. Now get out of here."

"Ok, I guess I understand," I stammered, I began to walk away, I turned and said, "just remember though, people change, and they grow. I was a bad person at one time, but I am not the same man I was. I am sorry for any pain I caused. Have a Merry Christmas, I love ya, always have, always will. I'm proud of the beautiful woman you have grown into. "

"Screw you old man, get lost, and take your damn picture with you." She yelled, as she threw the picture on the floor.

I tried to bend down, I couldn't make it.

"Let me get that for you mister." A voice said, I glanced over and saw a cute little girl running over to me, "My mommy is just having a bad day, sorry she dropped your picture." She said as she knelt down and handed me the picture.

"Why thank you young lady." I said.

She was quickly jerked away from me before she could tell me her name. "Get away from him, he's a bad old man, don't ever speak to him again young lady."

She drug her over to a large man, they both started looking and pointing at me.

The man looked at me and simply pointed towards the door.

My daughter got behind the counter and the crowd around us closing in, to get back in line. I stumbled away, lost in the crowd once again.

As I sat in front of Dawn, once again I found myself questioning my qualifications to be a parent to her child, just as I did Tara's child.

"Dawn, I don't know what kind of life our child would have had, it may not have been a good one, either way I should have been given a chance to have a say. The baby was still a part of me." I said.

"I know, I just didn't know what to do. Cassi suggested I should just take care of it, she said you are just a player and wouldn't care" Dawn said, as she wiped away the tears.

"Dawn, just because I am a player, doesn't mean I'm made of stone. Feelings are here. Why do you think men play? Deep down, many are looking for someone to love them. I may not spend a lot of time with my son, but when I do, and he is done crying because I took him from his mom, I have never felt a more complete love, I don't think I ever will."

"You already have a kid though, one you can't even take care of, so why would you want another anyway?"

"I guess it doesn't matter anymore does it." I said as I stood up, "since I didn't get to pay for the abortion, at least let me pay for your drink." I said as I threw a five on the counter. "Take care Dawn."

As I left the bar, I felt as though I was leaving my kid behind, even thought there was no kid there.

I went out that day and bought a toddler bed put it together and set it next to my bed, up until that point my son would sleep with me, or in my bed with me on the couch, now he had a place to sleep, he deserved it.

I called his mother the next day; I told her I needed to see him soon. I picked him up from his babysitters that afternoon and held him tighter than I ever had. I made up my mind then; I would never be a part of an abortion again.

As life went on, I moved around, had some heavy relationships, losses, gains, tears, laughter. I left my home town, enjoyed the city life for almost 4 years. Partied, drank, women, dancing all night that was my life for a while. I would still sit in bed some nights and think about what my kids might be doing now, it would pass though. I saw my son once a month or so, called him here and there, but he had a new step dad that was a big part of his life, I felt like I was interfering, he was a happy kid. My son became a big brother when his mom and new step dad gave birth to a baby girl. I worked at a busy Emergency room, I was on duty the day she gave birth, I must have called two dozen times, I felt like this child was partly mine too. She gave birth that evening, I was overjoyed, couldn't wait to see this new vision of loveliness. I made a special trip back home to visit, I was so happy for them; they had a real daughter, unlike the daughter I imagined.

Later that year I met a woman, we began an unhealthy relationship, when I tried to end it, she became psychotic, stalked me, punched me in the face, went a little nuts. That punch was my wakeup call; it was time to go back to the country. I needed to get back to my son.

A few months later, I moved back to my small rural home town, close to my dad, and most of all close to my son. I talked his mother into allowing me to have him every other week for one week. Took me a while, but I realized my fears as a young man, may not have been true, maybe I was not such a bad dad, maybe my kids would have been fine.

Then one day, my son and I walked into the local Kmart, and while walking down an aisle, I turned a corner, and bumped into a pretty lady, one I had not seen in years. It was Dawn. A rush of adrenaline hit me, I almost felt like running, but instead I froze.

"Hey you, how are you?" She asked, as she wrapped her arms around me.

"Great, wow, it's been what 10 years? Long time, great to see you, you look great." I stammered.

My son walked up behind me, "This is my son, Shawn, Shawn this is Dawn." I said.

My son extended his hand, "Hello."

"Nice to finally meet you Shawn." She said, as she shook his hand. I noticed a sparkle in her hand as she extended her arm.

"I see you are engaged, great, who's the lucky guy?" I said, as I pointed to the ring.

"He lives in San Diego, he's not from here, he comes up a few times a month. I am moving down there in a month to be with him."

"Wow, that's great, congrats." I replied.

"Thank you, he is a great guy, we have been together about 4 years."

"Hey maybe we could go to lunch today, we are almost done here, we could catch up?" I asked.

"Sure, sounds great." She replied. "Meet at the cottage?"

"Sounds good, we will be there in 15 minutes or so."

"See you there." She said, as she walked away, locking on to my eyes with her beautiful blues.

We met at the restaurant that afternoon, it was like we were old best friends, but the chemistry between us was so thick in the air you could cut it with a knife. She told me her fiancé was a great guy, and her son loved him, she was looking forward to marrying him, well actually her son was. She said he is stable, and makes good money, but really had nothing else to say about him. As she talked, I felt myself imagining our daughter again, a pretty young girl, 10 years old, with her eyes, her smile, her charm. I found myself gazing though Dawn....

"Dawn, I'm home baby. "I said, as I closed the front door.

"Hey daddy," my daughter said, as she came down stairs. "How was work?"

"Good honey how was school today?" I asked.

"Ok, I got into a little bit of trouble. I got detention."

"What? How did you do that sweetie? "I asked.

"This boy, he likes me and keeps bugging me in class, I told him to stop, but he wouldn't listen."

"Well they don't put you in detention for that, what did you do to make him stop?" I asked, in a gentle voice.

"I told him to piss off, sorry daddy, don't be mad please?" She said, as she grabbed my shoulders, holding on to me.

"Come here young lady, you aren't conning dad into letting you off this time, you are grounded." Dawn said as she pulled her off of me.

"Come on Dawn, she was defending herself, this creep should not have been screwing with her." I said, as I ran my hands through my little girl's hair.

"Tom, you can't let her charm you out of trouble every time, she is running you through the wringer, and you let her." Dawn said, as she gave me a kiss.

"She doesn't run me; I'm a tough dad, right pumpkin?" I asked as I swept my daughter up in my arms.

"You are the toughest dad!" She giggled, as I tickled her.

"You two are impossible, what am I gonna do with you?" Dawn asked.

"Love us till the end baby." I said.

As Dawn still continued about her life in the past 10 years, I listened to her, I continued the fantasy though, maybe this is our second chance, and maybe we could have the child we had given up years earlier.

Dawn and I spent the next few hours chatting, we parted ways and my son and I went home.

The next day, I got a phone call.

"Hello." I said.

"Tom, I called off my engagement." The voice on the other end said.

"Dawn? You did? Why?" I asked.

"I don't love him, I want you, I don't want him." She replied.

I felt overjoyed. That night she came over to my house, my son and I made her dinner, our attraction was off the charts powerful, we ended up having sex in the bathroom next to the kitchen while my son was making dinner. We spent the night together, it was magical. The years had passed, we had grown, and matured, maybe this second chance would work.

Dawn was having difficulty though; she had her son in her ear upset that she had broken off her engagement. A week after our first night back together, she called me to tell me she had become reengaged. She could not deal with the guilt. It hurt; I might not get this second chance. I asked desperately for us to meet. She said she couldn't, he was on his way up from San Diego, she could not contact me anymore.

I could see the social worker taking her off the horse again, taking her out of my life for good.

Two days later, Dawn called me; she wanted to meet, in public, so we could talk. We met at a park near my house.

"I'm so sorry I did this, I just can't do break this off, my son loves him." Dawn said.

"But do you love him?" I asked.

"No, I never have, but my son adores him. I figure I could be with him till my boy is an adult, then leave."

"My god Dawn, you know how awful that sounds?" I replied, "How is that fair to do to this guy?"

"I know, but it's my son, I only care about him."

"So you teach him it's ok to settle?"

"No, I don't want that, I want you, I love you." Dawn said.

"I love you Dawn." I said, although I knew in the back of my mind, I was using her for the same reason she was using her fiancé, the only difference is her son actually exists, and my future daughter was a fantasy.

We spent the next hour up in my room at my house, having sex like a couple of jack rabbits. In the back of my mind, I knew I wanted to try and get her pregnant again; this would be the second chance.

The next few weeks it killed me, he was staying with her, she would see me during the daytime, and him at night. When he left, she would invite me over to her house after her son would go to sleep, and she would let me stay the night, I would just have to stay in her room until they left in the morning.

This went on until finally one night she called me up.

"I'm done with him, I broke it off, we are through." Dawn said.

"Great! I love you that must have been hard. "I replied, overjoyed.

"It was, but I did it." She said.

The next month we were back to being inseparable, love was in the air. Then she dropped another bombshell again. With the pressure mounting from her son, she was getting back with him, and moving away.

She sobbed on the phone," I don't know why, I just can't handle the weight of my son's disapproval, it's too much. I love you Tom, but I love my son more." She cried.

"Dawn, this is the last time, you make this decision, but you make it in front of me."

"No, I can't, I can't see you again, and it's killing me."She said.

"Then I will go to your house, I'm on my way." I said as I hung the phone up.

I jumped up, and began to dress, the phone rang. I let the answering machine pick it up, Dawn said, "I'm on my way, stay there."

I sat on my couch, and waited for a few hours, then a knock at my door.

I opened it, there was Dawn, in her Pajamas, soaking wet from the rain, sobbing. "I don't know what to do."

"Well leaving with this guy is not the answer." I said as I pulled her inside. We lay in bed together talking, and having one final sexual encounter, I tried my hardest that night to get her pregnant, I knew this was the last chance I would have at my daughter I never had.

About 4am that morning, and after a few sexual escapades, Dawn walked out my front door, "I still love you Tom."

"I love you Dawn, but if you walk away now, don't ever contact me again, you will never see me again, understand? You have hurt me enough." Thinking in the back of my mind, she would call me sobbing the next day, or in a month telling me she is pregnant, and that we should be together. I mean she said it herself right, she loves her kids more than this guy or me. If she was pregnant, we would both get what we want.

Dawn walked away that night, I stood in the rain watching her drive away, and the thoughts of the family we could have had, the daughter I had fantasized about for many years, may have just died, again.

The next night, I kept the phone real close to me, hoping, praying, it didn't ring. The night after that, I put it in bed with me, hoping if it rang I would hear it, it didn't. After a week, I knew she had already moved, I drove by her place of employment, her car was not parked there anymore, I did that for the next few weeks, sat there and stared at the empty parking spot. My daughter, who never existed, was gone.

7.

Recollection

I hurt, very badly for a few months, depressed, lonely. But my son, who still lived with me half the time, brought me out of my funk, whether he meant to or not. Life went on, day in day out, new girlfriend, or two. Years went by. I dealt with the passing of my mother, and all my grandparents, getting married, and divorced for of all things my wife cheating on me. I never told my wife about these experiences, the pain was still there. I knew this woman would not make a suitable mother, so I never had it in mind to have children with her; we had 3 kids between the two of us that was enough. After my wife left, and the divorce was final, I once again bounced back as I always did. I ended up finding Dawn on Facebook, sent her a message, she replied. She had indeed moved away with that fella the week after our last meeting, she married and divorced him after only a year. She took a trip to Australia, and met a man there, they married and she was happy.

I was truly happy for her, sad for the life we may have had, but knew that I had to stop holding on to that.

Then a month or so after finding Dawn, I get a Facebook message, this time, it was from Tara.

Tara it turns out lived very close to me, only 20 minutes away, still a masseuse, had a live in boyfriend, no kids, still had not been married.

We made plans to meet up for breakfast at Brookfield's one morning after I got off duty at the firehouse, we met.

"Tara, hey sweetie, it's been too long." I said, as I gave her a big hug, "How are you?"

"I'm great Tom; it's so nice to see you." She hugged me back. She looked just about the same as she had looked 18 years earlier that was the last time we had even spoke. She told me her mother still lives in the same old house that she painted pink, her brother had died a few years back, and that it devastated her. Tara had been working at a local spa doing massage for the past few years, and that her boyfriend and her were on the outs, she figured it would end soon.

I filled her in about my life, how many twists and turns I had faced, the deaths, the triumphs, the son who I love dearly.

"Do you ever think about it Tara?"

"What? "She replied

"Our child? Ya know, what he would look like, what he would be doing, how much love he would have brought into our lives? "I replied.

"I try not to Tom, that's a painful memory. Not something I want to remember."

"I think about it Tara, it bugs me. I think about a son we may have had, I remember the type of father I thought I would have been back then, and the type of father I am now, I was delusional to not think I could handle it. I think now that I could have, I regret what we did."

Tara began to tear up, "We can't go back, we can't change the past. That's why I try and not think about it."

"I wish it was that easy for me Tara." I said, as I stared out the window. "Our son would be 18 now, a grown man, ready to take on the world."

Outside, I noticed a young man; he had a glowing smile on his face, a cap and gown on, a diploma in his hand. I saw myself walking up to him.

"Proud of you son, congratulations, you deserve it." I said, as I hugged the young man.

"Thanks dad, couldn't have done it without your support, you and mom are the best."

I turn, and there is Tara standing next to me, she puts her arm around me, looks up at me with a smile and says, "We did the right thing Tom, we made the right decision."

I knew deep down that these were just fantasies. It didn't mean that they may have not happened this way if given the chance. I will never know what my child with Tara or Dawn will look like, would they have been successful? Would they love me or hate me? Would one of them have grown up to be president? I don't think there is anything wrong with thinking about it, never forgetting what might have been.

I am turning 40 this year, my son will be 21. He now lives with me, he works two jobs, has a girlfriend. I think I have talked him out of the playboy lifestyle I once led. I hope he never has to be faced with this decision; I look forward to being a grandparent someday. I just might see a small piece of my children that never were, in my son's children that will be.

CPSIA information can be obtained at www.ICGtesting.com
Printed in the USA
LVOW07s2215090714

393593LV00001B/237/P

9 781482 606461